Norah's Ark

NORAH'S ARK

Jean E. Holmes

Review and Herald® Publishing Association
Washington, DC 20039-0555
Hagerstown, MD 21740

This book was
Edited by Raymond H. Woolsey
Designed by Dennis Ferree
Cover design by Bill Kirstein
Inside illustrations by Mary Bausman
Cover art by Denny Bond

Printed in U.S.A.

R & H Cataloging Service

Holmes, Jean E., 1941-
  Norah's Ark

    [1. Animals—Stories.   2. Christian life.]   I. Title.
                       590

ISBN 0-8280-0417-X

**Dedicated to
Katrina Janelle**

Contents

Norah's Birthday

Norah sat on her swing in the backyard. She pushed with her feet and made the swing twist round and round. Round and round went the long chains that hung from the tree branch. Round and round went Norah. She lifted her feet and stuck her legs out straight. The swing hung quietly for just a second. Then it started turning in the other direction. Faster and faster went the swing. Faster and faster went Norah.

When the swing finally stopped, Norah looked up into the branches of the tree. Now the tree was going round and round. Norah stood up and tried to walk, but the ground was going round and round too. Plop! Norah fell onto the ground with a thud.

Mother came running out to see what had happened to Norah. But Norah was not hurt. She was giggling. Little giggles started way down in her tummy and came bubbling up past her lips. Mother started to laugh too.

"Why were you whirling round and round on your swing?" asked Mother. "You made yourself so dizzy that you fell down."

"I was wishing," said Norah.

"Do you have to get dizzy to wish?" asked Mother.

"Sometimes it helps," giggled Norah. She was glad that Mother had come out to talk with her. She wanted to tell Mother about her wish.

"What are you wishing for?" asked Mother.

Norah knew Mother would ask that question. She rested her head on Mommy's lap and looked up into her face. Mommy was smiling.

"I've been 6 years old for a very long time, Mommy."

Mother nodded. "Why yes indeed," she said. "You have been 6 years old for 364 days. That is a very long time."

"I think it's about time for me to be 7," replied Norah.

"You are quite right," said Mother.

She lifted Norah back up to the seat of the swing. Norah held onto the long chains, and Mother pushed her. Back and forth went Norah.

"Will I finally be 7 tomorrow?" asked Norah as she swung back and forth.

"You will finally be 7 tomorrow," answered Mother. "Tomorrow is your birthday."

"Yippee!" shouted Norah. "Now I can have my wish!"

"But I still don't know what your wish is," replied Mother.

Norah dropped off the swing and looked up at Mother. "Don't you remember, Mommy? Don't you remember what Daddy promised me a long, long time ago?"

Mother looked worried. She could not remember what Daddy had promised Norah. "What did Daddy promise you a long, long time ago?" she asked.

"It was when I was just beginning to be 6," Norah reminded Mommy. "Johnny Smith had four baby hamsters." Norah paused and waited for Mommy to remember. "I asked Daddy if I could have a hamster. He said I had to wait until I was 7. He said I had to wait till I was old enough to care for it myself."

"Oh, yes, now I remember," said Mother.

"Do you think that Daddy remembers?" asked Norah.

"Perhaps we should remind him," answered Mother as she winked at Norah.

Norah and Mother waited for Daddy to come home from work to ask him about the wish. Norah helped set the table. Mother cooked a very good supper. When Daddy got home they all sat down at the table, and Daddy said grace. Then they all started eating supper. Norah kept looking at Mommy. She was afraid that Mommy had forgotten about the wish.

Mother smiled at Norah and winked. Daddy saw the wink and began to smile too. "I think you two have a secret," said

Daddy. "Could the secret have something to do with your seventh birthday, Norah?"

Norah began to giggle. Now Daddy winked at her. Norah knew that Daddy had a secret too. "Did you remember my birthday wish, Daddy?" asked Norah.

"Humm," said Daddy. "We will have to see about that tomorrow. Tomorrow is your birthday." Daddy winked at Mommy, and they both smiled.

When Norah awoke the next morning, a sunbeam was playing with the white daisies on her wallpaper. Norah smiled a slow waking-up sort of smile. Even the sunbeam seemed to be winking at her.

She jumped out of bed and hopped down the stairs two at a time. She didn't see Mommy. She didn't see Daddy. But she did see a big box on the dining room table. It was wrapped in pretty pink paper and had a big pink bow on the top. An envelope was stuck to the bow. The front of the envelope had letters on it. The letters spelled N-O-R-A-H.

Suddenly Daddy's head popped up from below the other end of the table. "Surprise!" laughed Daddy.

Then Mommy's head popped out from behind the kitchen door. "Surprise!" called Mommy.

Norah wanted to pull the pretty pink paper away from the box as quickly as she could. She wanted to see what was in the box. But Daddy said that she must read the card first.

"Oh, Daddy," complained Norah, "I don't read very well yet."

"Stuff and nonsense!" said Daddy. "What do the letters on the envelope say?"

Norah smiled. "They say Norah," she answered with pride.

"Of course you can read well!" said Daddy.

"I'll help you read the inside of the card," said Mommy. She sat down and lifted Norah onto her lap. Daddy handed them the card.

Mommy pointed to each word while Norah read. The card

said, "Norah's Ark. Happy Birthday From Mommy and Daddy."

Norah looked puzzled. "What does that mean?" she asked.

"Don't you remember the story of Noah's ark?" asked Daddy.

"Oh, of course I do, Daddy," answered Norah. It was one of her very favorite Bible stories.

"Well," said Daddy, "if you take the R out of the middle of your name, what do you have?"

Norah looked at the letters of her name very carefully. She was still puzzled. "I would have the letters N-O-A-H," she answered.

"There you are!" said Daddy with glee. "When you take the R out, you have N-O-A-H. That spells Noah, just like in the story of Noah and the ark!"

"Oh, Daddy," giggled Norah, "you're so funny!"

"OK, Miss Giggles," said Daddy, "now you may pull off the paper."

Norah grabbed the paper and ripped. She tore the paper off the front of the box. But the box was not made of cardboard. She could see through its sides. The box was made of glass. Lots of little wood shavings were on the bottom of the box. There was a little furry something in the corner of the box.

Now Norah pulled the paper off carefully. The little furry something had two little shiny black eyes and a funny little pink nose that wiggled back and forth. Norah could see two little pink feet sticking out from under the soft white and tan fur.

"A hamster!" shouted Norah. "Oh, I have my own hamster!"

Norah's shout scared the hamster. It jumped up and rolled onto its back with its little pink feet in the air. Then Norah saw the wood shavings under the hamster's resting place start to wiggle. Norah looked very closely. There were lots of tiny little pink things wiggling around on the wood shavings.

Norah's mouth opened wide. "Babies!" she whispered. "There are hundreds of little pink babies!"

"Not quite hundreds," laughed Mommy. "Thirteen is more like it. Daddy and I counted 13 babies."

"But why did you get one with so many babies, Daddy?" asked Norah.

Mommy looked at Daddy. Daddy looked sheepish and began to grin. "W-e-l-l," said Daddy with a long drawl, "she was the cutest hamster in the pet shop. She was roly-poly and furry. I bought her and the cage she was in. When I got home I put the cage in the closet."

Mommy began to laugh. "I'll finish the story. Daddy asked me to wrap your present after you went to bed. I looked down into the cage as I was wrapping it. I saw something wiggling down in a corner. Daddy had bought a cute roly-poly hamster. She was roly-poly because she was going to have babies. She had her babies last night!"

Daddy began to giggle. "I told Mommy that I wanted to buy you an ark of animals. It seemed like a pretty good start."

They all had a good laugh. And that was the beginning of Norah's Ark!

Patient Mother Raccoon

Norah's love for animals had started when she was just a tiny little girl. Both Mommy and Daddy loved animals, and they taught Norah to love them, too. Daddy was always bringing home stray or hurt animals. He and Mommy would do their very best to care for them or make them better. Other people brought hurt animals and baby birds to Norah's house. They knew that Norah's Mommy and Daddy would take good care of them.

There always seemed to be a baby bird that needed feeding, or a grown bird with a broken wing that needed mending. Sometimes there were baby squirrels that had to be fed a special milk formula from a little doll's bottle. Mommy kept all sorts of salves and bandages handy. She used soda straws to make splints for a bird's broken leg, a little box fitted with a heating pad and light bulb to keep newborns warm and cozy, and eyedroppers and cotton swabs to place medicines in just the right spots.

Norah loved to help Mommy nurse the little birds and animals. But sometimes it was a very sad job. One corner of the backyard was set aside as a special burial ground for the poor little creatures that Mommy could not help get better. Each time that they dug a tiny little grave, Mommy would talk to Norah about heaven. She told Norah that little birds and animals would never die in heaven. Norah wished that Jesus would come soon so she and Mommy and Daddy could live in heaven. She wanted to have a house with a big backyard when she got to heaven. She was glad that there would not have to be an animal cemetery in that backyard.

Mommy also taught Norah about the ways of little wild creatures. She told Norah that people could learn a great deal by watching birds and animals. One of the very best lessons, Mommy said, was the lesson of patience. Norah loved to listen to the stories Mommy told about the patience of animals. Her most favorite was the story of "Patient Mother Raccoon." Mother had first told her that story when she was very, very little. Now she still liked to crawl up onto Mommy's lap and say, "Tell me the raccoon story again, Mommy." Would you like to hear the raccoon story too? Well, here it is:

Mother Raccoon sat on the side of the road. Behind her sat four baby raccoons. Mother Raccoon was worried. She wanted to cross the road with her babies.

First Mother looked down the road. Then Mother looked up the road. Cars and trucks were speeding past. How could she get her babies across the busy road?

A woman who was driving the car down the road saw Mother Raccoon and her babies. She slowed down and stopped her car. She turned on her blinker lights to warn the cars coming down the road. She put her hand out the window to stop the cars coming up the road. All the cars and trucks stopped.

Mother Raccoon looked up and down the road. She saw that the cars and trucks had stopped. She turned and looked at her babies. "Churr-churr-churr," said Mother Raccoon. To her babies it meant "It is time to cross the road. Form a line and follow me."

Mother Raccoon walked across the road. One, two, three little raccoons followed her. They were all in a line. They looked straight ahead at Mother. Their brown-ringed tails stood straight in the air like little flags.

Mother got to the other side of the road. She counted her babies. One, two, three little raccoons stood by her side. Someone was missing!

"Wee-wee-wee," cried little raccoon number four. He was

still on the other side of the road. He was very frightened. Mother called to encourage him. But little raccoon number four was too frightened to cross the road alone.

Mother looked at the three little raccoons beside her. "Churr-churr-churr," she said, which must have meant "Follow me." Back across the road went Mother Raccoon. One, two, three little raccoons followed her. Their tails were straight in the air like little flags.

The woman in the car laughed. People in the other cars got out to see what was happening. They laughed too. Some drivers were not patient. They blew their horns and shouted. But the cars and trucks did not move.

Mother Raccoon talked softly to raccoon number four. She did not scold. She purred gently to him. "Purr-purr-purr," she said. She was probably telling him in raccoon language, "Be a brave, little raccoon, and follow me."

She started across the road again. One, two, three little raccoons followed her. Their tails stood straight in the air like little flags.

But little raccoon number four did not follow. He was frightened of the road. He was frightened of all the cars and trucks. The people laughed and called to little raccoon to cross the road. But he was frightened of the people. He sat on the side of the road and cried.

Baby raccoon number four cried, and Mother came back and licked his head. She grasped him gently in her mouth. Slowly she crossed the road with baby number four swinging back and forth from her mouth. One, two, three little raccoons followed behind. They looked straight ahead at Mother. Their little tails were straight in the air like little flags.

Jesus loves Mother Raccoon and all her babies. He put love and patience in her heart. That is why Mother Raccoon loved and helped baby number four.

Jesus loves boys and girls, too. He understands when they are frightened. He is patient with them and loves to help them. He made the little birds and animals. He wants us to be kind and patient as they are.

The Secret
in the Burrow

Norah's mother and father gave her a rabbit. Norah loved her rabbit and took good care of it. She kept it in a big cage in the backyard. Often she took her rabbit out of the cage and let it hop around the yard. The rabbit loved to hop around the yard. It loved to dig holes in the yard. It would dig very deep holes, called burrows, all over the backyard.

Norah fed her rabbit every morning and every evening. Every morning she took her rabbit out of the cage. She held and cuddled it, just as Mommy and Daddy held and cuddled her. Then she let her rabbit hop around the yard. Sometimes she saw little wild brown rabbits playing with her rabbit. She liked to watch them play. But she wanted her rabbit to be safe at night. Each evening she picked up her rabbit and put it back into the cage.

Norah's rabbit had a secret. It had a secret in one of the deep burrows in the backyard. Norah did not know that her rabbit had a secret. Mother and Father did not know that her rabbit had a secret.

One evening rain began to fall. Big drops of rain fell. *Plop, plop, plop*; the raindrops fell in the backyard. *Plop, plop, plop*; the raindrops fell on the burrow. *Plop, plop, plop*; the raindrops fell on the roof of the rabbit's cage.

Norah's rabbit was in the cage. Norah had seen the dark clouds coming and put her rabbit into the cage. She knew her pet was safe and dry.

The raindrops came down faster and faster. Soon there

were big puddles in the backyard. The puddles were near the burrow. The raindrops were falling into the burrow.

Norah's rabbit sat in its cage and looked at the burrow. It saw the rain falling into the burrow. It saw the puddles near the burrow getting bigger and bigger. The rabbit began to feel very frightened.

Norah's rabbit began to jump up and down in its cage. It thumped its hind feet hard on the floor of the cage. *Thump, thump, thump*, went its hind feet. It was very frightened!

Norah was in the house. She heard her pet thumping its hind feet in the cage. Norah knew that rabbits make that noise when they're frightened. Why was her rabbit so frightened? Was it afraid of the thunder and lightning? Was it afraid of the rain?

The rain came down harder and harder. The wind blew through the trees, making a swooshing noise. *Bang*! went a clap of thunder. Flash! went the lightning. The puddles in the backyard got deeper and deeper.

Norah's rabbit stood up on its hind feet. It stretched way up to the door on the top of the cage. It pushed the door up as far as it would move, again and again. *Clatter, clatter, clatter*! went the door.

Norah's mother heard all of the noise in the backyard. She called to Norah, "Why is your rabbit making so much noise? Why is she banging the door of her cage?"

"She must be frightened," said Norah. "She must be frightened of the thunder and the lightning. She must be frightened of the rain."

Mother looked at Norah. She looked at the pet rabbit in the big cage. She looked at the deep puddles in the backyard. Then she saw the burrow with the secret.

"Hurry, Norah!" said Mother. "Hurry and let your rabbit out of the big cage!"

"But why?" asked Norah. "She will get all wet."

"Hurry, Norah!" said Mother. "Your pet rabbit has a secret. The secret is in a burrow in the backyard."

Norah and Mother ran through the rain. They ran through

the puddles. Norah opened the door of the rabbit's cage.

Pop! Out jumped Norah's rabbit. It hopped quickly across the yard and disappeared into the burrow. Mother and Norah ran to the burrow. The rain was falling into the puddles. Water was going down into the burrow.

Mother knelt down by the burrow. She reached her arm way down into the hole. Then Mother started to smile. There was mud on Mother's arm and on her face. But Mother smiled right through the mud.

"Your pet rabbit has a secret down in the burrow," said Mother. "Would you like to see the secret?"

She pulled her arm out of the hole. A tiny ball of brown and white fluff was in her hand. The ball of fluff had two long ears and a tiny puffy tail. She put her arm down into the hole again. Out came another fluffy ball. Mother put her arm in the hole two more times. Each time that she pulled her arm out she had a fluffy little ball in her hand.

"Bunnies!" cried Norah. "Baby bunnies! That is the secret in the burrow!"

"Yes," said Mother. "Your pet rabbit is a mother. She was not afraid of the thunder and lightning. But she was afraid of the rain. She was afraid that the rain would drown her babies!"

"Oh, Mother," asked Norah, "how did you know there was a secret in the burrow?"

"I think Jesus helped me to know the secret," said Mother. "Jesus loves your mother rabbit and her baby bunnies. He did not want her babies to drown."

"Jesus is so kind!" said Norah. "I think we should thank Him for showing us the secret in the burrow."

Mommy and Norah knelt down in the mud by the burrow. Norah held the baby bunnies in her hands. Mother held Norah's rabbit. The rain was still falling. But Norah and Mommy did not mind the rain. They prayed to Jesus and thanked Him for saving the baby bunnies.

Mother Rabbit and Her Babies

P. S. Possum

A tiny little opossum came to Norah's Sabbath school class one day. He had a long pink tail. There was no hair on his tail. He had round pink-and-black ears. There was no hair on his ears. His eyes were tightly closed.

A kind woman brought the little opossum to Sabbath school. She had found him lying in her backyard. He was all alone. He had lost his mother.

Norah's mother was the Sabbath school class teacher. She loved little animals. The kind woman brought the little lost opossum to Norah's mother to take care of. The woman knew that Norah would help take care of the little lost opossum, too.

Norah looked at the opossum. "Mother," asked Norah, "when will the possum grow hair on his tail?"

Mother smiled. "Possums do not grow hair on their tails. He will always have a long pink tail with no hair."

Norah held the opossum very carefully and looked at him again. "Mother," asked Norah, "when will he grow hair on his ears?"

Mother began to laugh. "Possums do not grow hair on their ears. This little possum will always have pink-and-black ears with no hair on them."

Norah had a worried look on her face. She looked at the little opossum's eyes. They were tightly closed. The little opossum could not see with his eyes tightly closed. "Oh, Mother," asked Norah, "will the possum ever open his eyes? Will he ever be able to see?"

Mother smiled a great big smile and lifted Norah onto her lap. She gently took the little lost opossum from Norah. "This little possum will definitely open his eyes. Many baby animals, such as this little possum, are born with their eyes closed. But soon he will open his eyes and see the big world around him."

Norah sat on Mother's lap and watched the little opossum wiggling about in Mother's hand. It was so very tiny! "Mother," asked Norah, "why did this little possum get lost? Why did he lose his mother?"

Mother looked at the little opossum very closely. She looked at his back and his tummy. She looked at the top of his tail and the bottom of his tail. "I think I see the reason why this little possum got lost," said Mother. "I think I see the reason on his tail."

Norah rubbed the opossum's back with her finger. She looked at him very carefully. She looked at his back and she looked at his tummy. She looked at the top of his tail and the bottom of his tail. She saw a long, deep cut on the bottom of his tail.

"I see a cut on the possum's tail," said Norah.

Mother nodded.

"But why would a cut make him lose his mother?" asked Norah.

"A mother possum has two ways to carry her babies," said Mommy. "She has a pouch on her stomach. When her babies are born they crawl into the pouch. They stay in her pouch until they have fur on their bodies, everywhere but on their tail and their ears.

"The mother possum has a furry back and a long pink tail," continued Mommy. "There is no fur on her tail either. She can use her long pink tail to hold onto things. She can curl her tail forward and hold it over her back. When the baby possums are old enough to come out of the mother possum's pouch, they crawl up to her furry back. They hold on with their little paws. They use their long pink tails to help them hold on. Sometimes they even hold onto their mother's big pink tail with their little pink tails."

Norah laughed. That sounded cute. "I would like to see them holding onto their mother's tail with their little pink tails," she said. "But how did they learn to do that?"

"God created them that way," said Mother. "He created the mother possum with a pouch to carry her babies. He created the mother possum and her babies with long pink tails that help them hold on. He put love and care in the mother possum's heart and mind. That is why she knows how to take care of her babies."

Norah thought a moment. She looked at the little opossum again. "Oh," said Norah, "I know why this little possum lost his mother! He has a cut on his tail. He could not hold on tight. He fell off and got lost!"

"Maybe," said Mother. "But God loves this little possum. He helped the kind woman find the possum and bring him to us. Now we must be mothers to this little possum. We must love him and care for him. We must feed him and help him grow up to be a big possum. Then we can let him go back outside and live in the woods again. That is where big possums belong."

Mother and Norah took the little opossum home. They put him into a warm box with soft cotton. They fed him with a little doll's bottle.

Soon the little opossum opened his eyes. He could see Norah and Mommy. He crawled toward them and wanted to be held. He learned how to hold onto Norah with his long pink tail. He held onto one of Norah's fingers. Norah could walk around holding the opossum up in the air. It would swing back and forth, hanging upside down from her finger.

One day Norah brought the little opossum to Mother. "Mommy," she said, "we can not keep calling this possum little possum. He is starting to get big. He must have a name. What is a good name for this possum?"

Norah and Mother thought and thought. They thought of the name Pinky because he had pink ears and a pink tail.

"No," said Norah, "that is not a good name. A grown-up possum would not like to be called Pinky."

They thought of the name Fluffy.

"No," said Norah, "that is not a good name. His fur is not very fluffy."

Suddenly Mother smiled. "I know a good name," she said. "We can call him P. S. Possum!"

"P. S. Possum?" asked Norah. "That is a funny name. What does the P. S. mean?"

Mother laughed. "P.S. is what you put at the end of a letter when you've forgotten something that is important. This little possum was forgotten, and he is important. He is important to God and he is important to us."

"Oh, yes!" said Norah. "That is a good name. We will call him P. S. Possum because he is important!"

P. S.'s First Tree-climbing Lesson

Cuddle Time

Ready Robin
Is Ready

Two young boys brought a baby robin to Norah's house. It was a tiny baby robin. It did not have many feathers. It looked sick.

Mother and Norah put the little robin into a box with a heating pad under it and a little light over it. They put some soft cloth on the bottom of the box for the baby robin to snuggle in.

Then Mother mixed some special food for the robin. She put the food into an eyedropper and held it over the baby robin's mouth. The baby robin did not open his eyes. He did not see the food. He did not open his mouth.

Mother reached down and gently opened the baby robin's mouth. She put a tiny bit of food into his mouth. Then Mother gently rubbed his throat with the tip of her finger. The baby robin swallowed the food.

Every hour Mother fed the baby robin a tiny bit of food. Soon he began to open his eyes when Mother held the dropper near his mouth. He blinked his little black eyes at Mother and opened his mouth. He opened it very, very wide.

Norah learned how to feed the baby robin. She and Mother awoke when the sun first peeped over the trees. They fed the baby robin little bits of food all day long. When the sun began to set behind the trees, they placed a cover over the top of the baby robin's box. He closed his eyes and went to sleep. Norah did not have to feed the baby robin then. Norah closed her eyes and went to sleep too.

After a few days the baby robin began to wake up before

the sun peeped over the tops of the trees. "Chirp, chirp, chirp," he said, as if to say, "I am hungry. Come feed me, Norah!"

Norah rubbed her eyes and stumbled out of bed. She lifted the lid off the baby robin's box and fed him. She fed him a little bit every hour, all day long.

"Mother," said Norah one day, "it is hard work being a parent to a baby bird. Baby birds are always hungry!'

"Yes," said Mother. "Mommy and daddy robins have to scurry about all day long to find food for their babies. They are very busy birds!"

Mother and Norah gave the baby robin a name. They named him Ready Robin. Ready Robin was a good name because he was always ready to eat.

Ready Robin began to grow big and strong. He sat up on the edge of his box and chirped at Norah and Mother.

Ready Robin began to grow feathers. The feathers on his breast were soft and red. The feathers on his wings and tail grew long. He liked to twitch his tail and flap his wings. He sat on Norah's finger and flapped his wings up and down. Norah put him onto her shoulder. Ready flapped his wings up and down. Norah giggled because his feathers tickled her ear.

"Norah," said Mother, "I think Ready wants to fly. Shall we teach him?"

"Oh, Mother!" laughed Norah. "We can't teach Ready how to fly!"

"Why not?" asked Mother.

Norah giggled some more. "We can't teach Ready to fly because we don't know how to fly!"

Mother giggled too. "We don't have to fly to teach Ready. We just have to give him a shove. Jesus gave Ready wings and feathers. Ready is built to fly. He just doesn't know it yet."

Mother and Norah took Ready outside. They stood in the middle of the yard. Mother placed Ready on her hand and held him up in the air. "OK," said Mother. "Are you ready to fly, Ready Robin?" She suddenly dropped her hand. Ready Robin fluttered to the ground and went *plop*!

"That wasn't very good flying!" said Norah. "Are you sure that Ready is ready to fly, Mother?"

"Oh, yes," said Mother. "He just needs a few more lessons."

"He certainly does!" said Norah.

Mother lifted Ready up in the air again. "Are you ready?" asked Mother.

"Chirp, chirp, chirp," said Ready Robin.

This time Mother gently threw Ready up into the air. He flapped his wings up and down. Flap, flap, flap, went Ready's wings. Plop went Ready down to the ground!

"Maybe that's enough flying lessons for today," said Mother. She and Norah took Ready back to his box. But Ready didn't want to stay in his box. He wanted to ride around on Norah's shoulder.

Mother and Norah took Ready out into the yard every day for flying lessons. Soon he learned to glide down to the ground instead of plopping onto the ground.

"Now Ready must learn to eat worms," said Mother.

Norah's eyes grew very large. "How will he learn to eat worms, Mother?"

"We will teach him," said Mother.

"Oh, no!" said Norah. "How can we teach him to eat worms? We don't eat worms, Mother!"

Mother laughed. "Come on, Norah. Let's go out to the garden and find some worms." Mother placed Ready on Norah's shoulder. "Come along," said Mother.

Mother got down on her hands and knees and dug in the dirt. Soon she found a wiggly little worm. Norah wrinkled up her nose at the worm. "Who is going to eat that wiggly little worm first?" asked Norah.

Mother laughed again and hugged Norah. "Why, Ready Robin will eat the worm," she said. "People don't eat worms!"

Norah heaved a great sigh of relief.

Mother placed Ready on the ground. She held the wiggly worm over his head. Ready opened his mouth very wide. Gulp! Down went the wiggly worm into Ready's tummy.

"Now Ready must learn to find his own worms," said Mother. She dug around in the dirt again. Soon she spotted another little wiggly worm. She placed Ready on the dirt near the worm. "Are you ready to catch that worm, Ready Robin?" asked Mother.

Ready's little black eyes flashed. He turned his head to one side and looked at the wiggly little worm. Peck! went Ready Robin. The worm disappeared into his tummy.

All summer Ready Robin stayed with Norah and her family. He didn't live in the box anymore. Now he perched on a limb of the big maple tree in the backyard. He slept up in the tree all night long.

Mother had a clothesline in the backyard. It was a pulley line. A little wheel was attached to the outside of the kitchen window. Another little wheel was attached to the trunk of the maple tree. The clothesline stretched from the window to the tree and went around the two little wheels.

Each morning Ready Robin hopped off his limb of the tree onto the clothesline. Mother would open the kitchen window and pull the line in. Ready Robin rode on the clothesline all the way to the window. Then he would hop off onto the sill and chirp for his breakfast.

Autumn came, and the leaves of the maple tree began to turn the same color as the feathers on Ready Robin's breast. "Soon Ready Robin will be ready to leave," said Mother.

"Where is he going?" asked Norah.

"He is going south for the winter," said Mother. Mother was right. Soon Ready did not ride on the clothesline anymore. Ready had gone south.

Winter came and went. It was spring again. Little red buds began to pop out all over the maple tree. One day Norah opened the kitchen window to look at the pretty red buds. There sat a big robin with a red breast on the end of the clothesline. Ready Robin had come home!

Norah and Baby Bird

The Piano Mice

Not all of the little creatures that came to live in Norah's home were welcome houseguests. Some came in quite uninvited. Mother and Daddy loved birds and animals, but they always taught Norah that God had created the beautiful outdoors for wild animals to live in. That was true for big wild animals, of course. But it also was a good rule for even very tiny wild animals. The piano mice helped Norah to understand the difference between "indoor" animals and "outdoor" animals.

Mother and Norah went looking for a piano. They went to several piano stores and saw many different pianos. Norah thought that all of the pianos were pretty. Mother thought that all of the pianos were expensive.

They told Daddy about the pianos they had seen. Mother told him how expensive they were. Daddy sat and thought for a few moments. Then he began to smile. "I have an idea," he said. "Let's look for a secondhand piano."

They looked for a secondhand piano for two weeks. Daddy read newspaper ads. Mother made many phone calls. One day Daddy came home with a big smile on his face.

"I have found a secondhand piano," said Daddy. "The wood is old and scratched, but I can paint it. It is very big and heavy, but I'll get help to move it. It is old and it is big, but it sounds very nice."

Mother and Norah were excited when the piano arrived. Norah sat down on the piano bench and began to try to play. *Bong, bong, bong, bing, bing, bing,* went the piano.

"That sounds very nice," said Mother, "but you must learn how to play songs. We will find a piano teacher for you, and she will teach you to play many pretty songs."

Norah started taking piano lessons. Her piano teacher

taught her to read musical notes. She taught her how to place her hands on the piano keys. She also showed her how the piano worked. The teacher lifted up the top of the piano and showed her all the tight wire strings. She showed her the little wooden hammers covered with felt.

Norah watched the inside of the piano as the teacher moved the keys. "Oh," said Norah. "I see how it works! Each little hammer hits its own wires. The wires make the pretty sounds."

Norah took piano lessons all through the winter. She took piano lessons all through the spring. She learned to play many pretty songs.

When summer came Daddy said, "It's time to take a vacation. We are going to take a nice trip. We will be gone for three weeks."

Their vacation trip was fun, but Norah was glad when they pulled into their own driveway again. She wanted to see all her animals. She wanted to start playing the piano again. She sat down on the piano bench and began playing her piano. *Ping, bing, bong!* went the piano. It sounded awful! There were no pretty sounds anymore! What had happened to her piano?

"Oh, Daddy!" wailed Norah. "Something awful has happened to my piano while we were on vacation! Listen, Daddy, it sounds just awful!" She played a few notes on the piano as she talked. Daddy looked very surprised.

Daddy opened the top of the piano and looked inside. "Uh, oh!" he said. "Look down into this piano, Norah. Look at what has happened to the little hammers."

Norah peeked inside the piano, and her mouth opened wide. She saw the little wooden hammers and she saw the long metal wires. But there was something wrong with the little hammers. There was no felt on the hammers. Some of the hammers even had little pieces of wood missing from them. They looked chewed. Norah touched them and looked up at Daddy. "What happened to these hammers?" she asked.

Daddy shook his head. "I don't know," he said, "but I'm

going to find out." He got down on the floor and opened the bottom of the piano. He poked his head inside and looked.

"Get me the flashlight, Norah," he said. Daddy shined the flashlight around inside the bottom of the piano. Norah could hear him making little muffled sounds. Then he pulled his head out and looked at Norah.

"Norah," he asked, "do you have any little brown gerbils?"

Norah shook her head back and forth.

"Do you have any little brown hamsters?"

Norah shook her head back and forth.

"Norah, do you have any little brown mice?"

Norah shook her head again.

Daddy took one more look inside of the piano. "Well," he said, "maybe you do not have any pet mice, but your piano does!"

"Mice!" shouted Norah. "How can my piano have pet mice?"

"Your piano has become a mouse house," said Daddy. "A family of field mice has come to live in your piano. It is a very big family. The mice have chewed the felt off the hammers to make themselves a nice soft nest. Now they are busy chewing through the little wooden hammers."

"Oh dear!" said Norah. "What shall we do? We can't let them chew up my whole piano!"

Daddy rested his chin on his hands and began to think. "We could put some poison in the piano," he said.

"Oh no!" said Norah. "We can't poison them, Daddy!"

Daddy thought a few moments longer. "We could put a mousetrap in the piano," he said.

"Oh, Daddy! No!" said Norah in a very worried voice. "We can't hurt them, Daddy. Mice are too cute."

"Mice are cute in a cage," said Daddy. "And mice are cute outdoors. But mice in a piano are not cute!" Daddy thought a moment longer. "We shall have to ask them to live someplace else."

"But how do you ask a mouse to move?" asked Norah.

"I think I know," answered Daddy. "But I will need some help."

Daddy asked some neighbors to come and help him move the field mice. Three strong men came to help. They all pushed and pulled on the big, heavy piano. They rolled it across the living room floor. They pushed it carefully out the front door. They rolled it across the porch. Mother opened the screen door of the porch.

"OK," said Daddy. "Now I want everyone to bang his hands on the piano. I want everyone to stamp his feet and shout loudly."

Mother and Norah and Daddy and the three other men did as Daddy said. They banged on the piano. They stamped their feet. They shouted loudly.

Some people walking down the street heard all the noise. They stopped to see what was going on. They saw Mother and Norah and four grown men banging on a piano and stamping their feet and shouting.

But the mice did not come out. They were afraid of the noise. They huddled in the back corner of the piano.

"This is not working very well," said Norah as she looked at the little mice huddled in the piano.

"No," said Daddy. "We have to think of something else."

Daddy sat down and thought some more. The three neighbors sat down to help him think. Suddenly one of the neighbors jumped up. "I have an idea!" he said. "We must make this piano a very uncomfortable place to live! We must turn this mouse house upside down and shake it back and forth. We must bang and stamp and shout."

By now a small crowd of people had gathered on the street to watch. They saw four grown men struggling to turn a very big piano upside down. Then the men started to shake the piano and shout. Mother and Norah banged on the piano and shouted.

Suddenly little field mice began to jump out of the piano. They ran around the porch in all directions. Mother and Norah ran after them and tried to chase them out the door.

Daddy and the neighbors banged on the piano and shouted.

One by one the little mice found the door and ran outside. After a while there were no mice running around. There were no mice in the piano.

The people in the street were laughing and clapping. Mother and Norah began to laugh. Daddy and the three neighbors began to laugh.

"Well," said Norah when she could catch her breath, "this is the funniest moving day I have ever seen!"

"Yes," chuckled Mother, "a piano is not a good house for field mice. Field mice are supposed to live outdoors in fields. Jesus created fields and little brown field mice to live in them."

Quincy Quacker

Norah," called Mother, "I have a surprise for you. Come and see if you can guess what the surprise is."

Mother was holding her hands behind her back. The surprise was in her hands. "This is a very special surprise," said Mother. "It is a surprise in a small package that is not quite round. But you cannot open this package. If you open it you will spoil the surprise. The surprise inside has to open the package itself."

Norah looked at Mother with a very funny look. She knew that Mother wanted her to guess a riddle. Mother liked to ask riddles. But Norah could not think of an answer to this riddle. She put her chin in her hands and thought. She stood on one leg and thought. But she could not think of an answer to the riddle.

"Give me some more hints, Mother," said Norah. "I need some more hints to help me guess this riddle."

"OK," said Mother. "I will give you a few more hints."

Norah sat down on the floor. Maybe she could think better if she sat down.

"This surprise is in a small white package," said Mother. "The outside of the package is hard, but it breaks easily. The inside is soft and squashy. The inside is not very pretty now. But if you keep this package safe and warm, the inside will become very pretty. The inside will change to something warm and soft."

Norah looked very puzzled. She could not guess what this surprise was. "Oh, Mommy, I cannot guess what this surprise is. Please show it to me."

Mother pulled her hands from behind her back. She showed Norah the surprise.

Norah looked very disappointed. "An egg!" cried Norah. "This is just an old, silly egg!"

"Oh no," said Mother. "This is not an old egg. It is a new egg. It was laid just this morning. And this is not a silly egg. It is a duck egg. Duck eggs are not silly."

"But what makes it so special?" asked Norah.

"It is special because we are going to help it hatch into a duck," said Mother. "Have you ever watched an egg hatch?"

"No," said Norah. Now Norah was getting curious. Mother had a way of getting Norah curious about things. She had never seen an egg hatch, but watching one hatch sounded like fun.

"Mommy," said Norah with a puzzled look on her face, "you and I have mothered baby birds and baby animals. We know how to feed and take care of baby robins and baby possums. But how can we mother an egg? How can we feed and care for an egg?"

Mother laughed. "It is quite easy when you know how," she said. "We do not have to feed the egg. The inside of this egg will change from something squashy to something soft and pretty by feeding on food already in there. God created this egg with just enough food inside to feed the little duck until he is ready to come out."

Norah looked very pleased. It was hard work to feed little birds. She was glad that God had food inside to feed the little duck egg for her.

"But what do we have to do for this egg to take care of it?" Norah asked. "Do we put it in the refrigerator with the eggs you bought when you went shopping?"

"Oh no!" laughed Mother. "We do not want this egg to get cold. It will not hatch if it gets cold. We want to keep this egg warm. Do you know how a mother duck keeps her eggs warm?"

"Oh yes," said Norah. "I know that. The mother duck sits on them. That is how she keeps them warm. Do we have to sit on this egg, Mother?"

"No," chuckled Mother. "We would break this egg if we sat

on it. Besides, it would take an awful lot of sitting! Would you want to sit on this egg for 30 days? That is how long a mother duck must sit on an egg to get it to hatch."

"Oh dear," said Norah. "I do not want to sit on this egg for 30 days! But how will we get it to hatch? How will we keep it warm and keep it from breaking?"

"That is another part of the surprise," said Mother. "Come into the garage with me, Norah. Come and see what I have."

Mother and Norah went into the garage. Norah saw a big white thing on the workbench. It looked something like a wheel. "What is this funny thing?" asked Norah.

"This is called an incubator," said Mother. "Can you say that big word, Norah?"

Mother helped Norah say the word *incubator*. Then she showed Norah how it worked. She showed her the electric cord coming out of the bottom. She showed her a metal wire on the inside. "This metal wire heats up just like the wire inside a toaster," said Mother. "But the incubator doesn't get as hot as a toaster. It gets just warm enough to keep the egg at the right temperature."

Norah saw a lot of ridges on the bottom of the incubator. A wire screen sat over the top of the ridges. Mother told Norah that they would put a little bit of water in the bottom between those ridges. "That will keep the egg from drying out," said Mother. "If the egg dries out, the duck will not hatch. The egg sits on the wire screen over the water."

Norah saw a little window in the top of the incubator. "What is this window for, Mother?" asked Norah.

"That is so we can watch the egg," said Mother. "It is so we can see the egg without having to lift the top off the incubator."

"Do we have to take the top off the incubator some-times?" asked Norah.

"Yes," said Mother. "We have to take the top off twice a day. We take the top off in the morning and turn the egg over. Then we take the top off in the evening and turn the egg over again."

"What if we forget?" asked Norah.

"That would not be good," answered Mother. "This egg needs to be turned over twice a day or the little duck will not hatch. A mother duck does that for her eggs. She stands up and uses her bill to roll the eggs over. We will have to lift the top and use our fingers to turn the egg over."

Norah began to look worried. She was glad that God would feed the little duck while it was growing in the egg. But hatching the egg was not going to be very simple. "What if we get mixed up? What if we forget to turn the egg? What if the egg rolls around?"

"Those are a lot of what-ifs!" said Mother. "But you are quite right. We could get mixed up. I will show you a way to help us remember."

Mother took a felt-tip pen. She marked an X on one side of the egg and an O on the other side. Then she and Norah made a chart. The chart had lines for 30 days. She told Norah that they would mark an X on the chart each morning when they turned the egg to the X side. Then they would mark an O on the chart each evening when they turned the egg to the O side.

Norah and Mother gently placed the duck egg on the wire screen in the incubator. They poured a little bit of water between the ridges in the bottom. They put the top on the incubator and turned the switch to 101 degrees. Then they taped their chart on the wall above the incubator.

Every morning Norah and Mother turned the duck egg over and marked the chart. Every evening they turned the egg over and marked the chart. They watched the water in the bottom and added a little bit every few days so the egg would not dry out. They watched the temperature to make sure that it was just right.

One morning Mother looked at the chart. "This is the twenty-sixth day," said Mother. "Now we will stop turning the egg for a few days. We will watch the egg through the little window. We will watch to see if it is going to hatch."

Mother and Norah watched the egg on the twenty-seventh day. It did not hatch. They watched it on the twenty-eighth day and twenty-ninth day, but it did not hatch. They watched it on the thirtieth day, but it still did not hatch.

"Oh, dear," said Norah, "maybe we did something wrong. Maybe our duck is not going to hatch."

"Let's wait another day," said Mother.

They waited another day, but it did not hatch. Mother told Norah that they would still wait another day. But the egg did not hatch. Mother began to look worried. She wanted Norah to see the little duck hatch out of the egg. But maybe the little duck was dead. Maybe they had done something wrong. Mother decided to wait just one more day.

On the thirty-third day Norah and Mother watched the egg very closely. They did not see the egg move, they did not hear little sounds coming from the egg. Mother waited until Norah's bedtime. She and Norah felt very sad.

Mother pulled the incubator's electric plug from the wall outlet. She took the top off the incubator and picked the egg up. Norah was in bed, but she was not asleep. She could hear Mother in the garage. She knew what Mother was doing. Norah began to cry. Little salty tears trickled down the side of her nose.

Mother walked over to the garbage can with the egg. She lifted the lid and was about to drop the egg into the plastic bag inside. Suddenly Mother stopped. She held the egg up to her ear. Mother's eyes opened wide. Her mouth opened wide.

"*Norah!*" Mother called as she came running in from the garage. "Get up, Norah! Come out to the garage quickly."

Norah jumped out of bed and ran to the garage. Mother held the egg up to Norah's ear. Norah's eyes opened wide. Her mouth opened wide. Norah heard a sound coming from the egg. The sound went "Peep-peep-peep."

Mother quickly put the egg back into the incubator and plugged in the electric cord. Then she and Norah watched through the little window. They saw a tiny crack in one side of the egg. Soon a tiny hole opened in the middle of the crack.

Norah could see something wiggling around on the other side of the hole.

Gradually the hole got bigger and bigger and the eggshell got more and more cracks. Norah and Mother watched the eggshell fall apart. Out came a wet little something. It did not look like a duck. It was wet and wrinkled-looking.

"Is that funny-looking thing going to be a duck?" asked Norah.

"Yes," said Mother. "He just needs to dry out a little. The warmth in the incubator will help him to dry out. Soon he'll be soft and fluffy."

Mother was right. Soon a little duck sat in the incubator. His feathers were brown and soft. He had a tiny bill and tiny little webbed feet. Mother told Norah that this duck was called a Muscovy duck.

Norah thought that her duck needed a better name. Muscovy was too hard to say. She and Mother gave her duck a cute name that was easy to say. They named him Quincy Quacker.

Quincy grew up to be a beautiful duck. His feathers looked shiny green in the sunlight. Norah "taught" him how to swim in the swimming pool in her backyard. She made a little wooden raft for Quincy with a pretty red sail on it. Quincy sailed around the pool on his raft when he was little. Sometimes he jumped into the water and swam to Norah. Then he jumped to the top of her head and rode around while she swam. When Quincy got big he lived in a pond with other ducks. But Norah knew that he was not like other ducks. Quincy Quacker was a special surprise!

Quincy's Raft

His Maiden Voyage

Hitching a Ride

"Look, Ma, I can fly!"

Jimmy, Jack, and Jennifer

The sun was nearly ready to set. Norah and her family were getting ready for Friday night worship. Soon the Sabbath would begin, and they wanted to be ready. It was a quiet and peaceful evening.

Suddenly the phone began to ring. *Ring-ring-ring* went the phone. Mother ran to answer it. "Uh, oh," said Daddy. "I have a sneaky sort of feeling that worship will be short this evening."

Mother came back into the living room. She had a rushed sort of look on her face. "Worship will have to be short this evening," she said.

Daddy winked at Norah.

Mother sat down and lifted Norah onto her lap. "We will have to take a ride after worship," said Mother.

Daddy smiled. "Let me guess. Is it a hurt bird?"

"No," said Mother. "This is not an 'it.' This is a 'them.' There are more than one."

"Uh, oh," said Daddy. "Are these baby raccoons?"

"No," said Mother. "You guessed wrong again."

"I give up," said Daddy. "Tell us why we have to take a ride. Tell us what we are going to get."

"Squirrels," said Mother with a worried look on her face. "Three tiny squirrels fell out of their nest. They are very, very young. Their eyes are not open yet. One of them is badly hurt."

"How did the squirrels fall out of their nest, Mother?" asked Norah. She knew that mommy and daddy squirrels build good nests. She knew that mother squirrels take good care of their babies.

"It was an accident," answered Mother. "Mrs. Andrew's husband was cutting down a pine tree this afternoon. It was a tall pine tree. He did not see the squirrel's nest at the top of the tree. The baby squirrels were shaken out of the nest when the tree began to fall. They fell a long distance and landed in some tall grass. The grass helped to soften their fall a little. But one of the babies was hurt badly."

Norah's family had a short worship. They thanked Jesus for the Sabbath. They asked Him to be with their family and keep them safe. They asked Jesus to help them know how to take care of the little squirrels. Then they got into the car and drove to Mr. and Mrs. Andrew's home.

Mrs. Andrew and her two children were waiting for Norah's family. The Andrews had tried to feed the little squirrels some milk. But the baby squirrels would not eat.

Mother picked up each little squirrel, one at a time. She looked at them very carefully. Two of the babies seemed to be all right. She put them into a box with some soft cotton in the bottom. The little squirrels pushed around into the cotton until they were all covered up. They seemed to like the cotton. They went to sleep.

When Mother put the third little squirrel into the box, he did not move around on the cotton. He lay very still. He was badly hurt. Mother picked him up and saw some blood on his tummy. She moved him very gently and saw that one of his back legs was broken. Mother placed him back down on the cotton. She had a worried look on her face.

"This baby squirrel is hurt badly, Norah," said Mother. "There is some blood on his tummy. He must be bleeding someplace inside his tummy. His back leg is broken. He is a very sick little squirrel."

"Can you make him better, Mommy?" asked Norah with pleading eyes. "Can you fix his leg and his tummy?"

Mother looked sad. "I can set his back leg, and it might be all right. I can put some medicine on the outside of his tummy where I see the blood. But I don't know if his tummy will get better. Jesus can help me to know how to set the little squirrel's leg. But, Norah," said Mother with a serious look on her face, "only Jesus can heal the inside of the squirrel's tummy."

"Let's pray right away!" said Norah. "Let's ask Jesus to fix the inside of the squirrel's tummy."

"Yes," said Mother, "we will pray and ask Jesus to heal the little squirrel. But, Norah, sometimes Jesus says no. Sometimes it's better if badly hurt little animals just go to sleep and never wake up again. We would not want this little squirrel to suffer, would we, Norah?"

"No," said Norah in a small voice. There were tears in her eyes. "I don't want this little squirrel to suffer. I don't want him to die, either. It is a very hard choice, Mother."

"We will pray to Jesus," said Mother. "We will ask Jesus to make the choice. Jesus will make the right choice. He will do what is best for this little squirrel."

After they prayed for the little squirrel, Norah's family got back into the car and drove home. They took the box with the little squirrels with them.

Mother set the hurt baby's leg as soon as they got home. She put some medicine on the outside of his tummy. The little squirrel did not move.

"Is he dead, Mother?" asked Norah. "He is not moving."

"No, he is not dead," answered Mother. She showed Norah that the baby's tiny chest was still moving up and down. "That means that he is still breathing," said Mother. She placed the tip of Norah's finger very gently on the baby's chest. Norah felt a tiny thumping sort of feeling. "That is his little heart beating," said Mother.

Then Mother prepared a special formula of milk. She warmed the milk and poured it into a doll's bottle. She gently lifted one of the baby squirrels that did not seem to be hurt. Very carefully she pushed the nipple of the bottle into the baby's little pink mouth. But nothing happened. The baby squirrel would not suck on the nipple. He would not drink the warm milk.

Mother gently stroked his throat and the side of his mouth with the tip of her finger. She squeezed the bottle just a tiny bit to push some of the milk into the baby's mouth. But the little squirrel would ot swallow it. The drop of milk rolled out of the side of his mouth.

"Oh dear!" said Norah. "What will we do? None of the babies will live if they don't drink the milk!"

"We will try a little trick," said Mother. In a pan, she added a small spoonful of honey to the milk and stirred it in. Then she put some of the milk with the honey in it into the bottle. She squeezed a few drops of the milk out onto one of her fingers. Then she gently opened the little squirrel's mouth and rubbed the drops of milk onto his tiny pink tongue. The little tongue began to move around. Mother put more milk onto her finger and rubbed it onto the baby's tongue. Finally she put the nipple of the bottle back into the little squirrel's mouth and squeezed the bottle just a tiny bit.

Norah watched closely. She saw the little squirrel's tummy go up and down. She saw a little bubble move slowly up through the milk in the bottle. "What's happening, Mother? What is happening to the squirrel?"

"He's drinking!" said Mother with a happy grin on her face. "He is drinking the milk!"

Mother had to do the same thing with the second little squirrel. This was a little girl squirrel. She wanted milk with honey in it too. She soon began to suck on the nipple hungrily. Mother knew that this little girl squirrel was going to be all right.

When it was time to feed the hurt little squirrel, Mother did not use the bottle. She held the hurt baby very carefully in a soft piece of cotton. She put a drop of milk onto her finger and rubbed it onto the squirrel's tongue. The little squirrel moved its tongue, and the drop of milk disappeared. Mommy kept feeding the hurt baby with her finger until he went to sleep.

The next morning Norah ran down to look at the baby squirrels. She saw them all snuggled up under the cotton in one corner of the box. They had rolled themselves up into little balls. When she pushed down the cotton, all three squirrels began to squirm around. Even the little hurt squirrel was moving around. He looked as though he felt better. Norah had a feeling that Jesus had healed her little hurt squirrel.

By the end of one week the little squirrels' eyes had opened. They sucked greedily on the nipple of the bottle. Mother had to buy two more bottles. The little squirrels were not very patient. They all wanted to be fed at the same time. Mommy and Daddy and Norah sat in the living room. They each had a little squirrel. They each had a little bottle. When Daddy was at work Mommy had to feed two squirrels at the same time. She set the alarm clock to awaken her in the middle of the night so she could feed the squirrels.

Norah named the three little squirrels Jimmy, Jack, and Jennifer. They followed Norah around the yard. They climbed up her clothes and sat on her shoulders. They especially liked to crawl into her pockets and go to sleep.

When they grew older, Norah fed her squirrels peanuts. Jimmy, Jack, and Jennifer ate some of the peanuts, but they did not eat all of them. Squirrels like to bury peanuts outdoors. But Norah's squirrels did not bury their peanuts in the yard. They buried them in Mother's potted plants. They buried them in the sofa and the chairs. They buried them all over Norah's house.

"Squirrels do not belong in a house," said Daddy one night when he found a peanut buried in his paper. "Squirrels belong in a tree."

Norah and Mother tried to teach Jimmy, Jack, and Jennifer to stay out in a tree. They put them up in the tree and then ran inside. They locked the door of the screened-in porch. Jimmy, Jack, and Jennifer thought that this game was fun. They scampered up the screens and tried to find a way in. When they could not find an open door, they tore a hole in the screen and came in.

"Having an ark of animals is not always very easy!" said Daddy. He fixed the hole in the screen. The next day there were two holes in the screens.

Mother and Norah started feeding the squirrels outside. Norah and Mother placed the peanuts on the ground under the tree. Jimmy, Jack, and Jennifer picked up the peanuts, tore their way through the screens, and buried the nuts in one of Mommy's potted plants.

All that summer Mommy, Daddy, and Norah tried to outsmart the three pet squirrels. They put the peanuts far out in the backyard. They put wire mesh over the screens. They put all of Mommy's potted plants out by the garden. Nothing worked. Jimmy, Jack, and Jennifer were certain that they lived inside of Norah's house.

The next spring the problem was finally solved. Jimmy, Jack, and Jennifer solved it themselves. The squirrels were grown now and wanted their own families. But their mates lived in trees. They did not live in Norah's house. Jimmy, Jack, and Jennifer decided to live out in the trees with their own little squirrel families.

Feeding Time

Learning to Eat Peanuts

Mother checks out the strength of Jack's newly healed leg.

Three tired squirrel babies cuddle up for a nap next to Norah.

Weasel Finds His Way

Norah awoke to the sound of funny little scratching, squeaking, and grunting noises. She lay very quietly and listened, trying to guess where the noises came from. They didn't sound like the noises her pet gerbils made. They made scratching and squeaking noises, but they didn't make grunting noises. The noises didn't come from her pet hamster. He made scratching and squeaking noises, but he didn't make grunting noises.

Norah slowly searched the room with her eyes. She spotted a cardboard box on the floor near the door. The top of the box was taped down tight, but someone had punched little round holes in the top and sides. The box was rocking back and forth. Something in it was making funny little scratching, squeaking, and grunting noises.

Norah tiptoed from her bed toward the box. The box stopped rocking. Everything was very quiet. Norah put an eye up close to one of the holes and peeked in. She saw a little pink eye peeking back out at her. Norah jumped back with a start! She had never seen anything with little pink eyes before. She had seen animals with black eyes and brown eyes and even blue eyes. But she could not imagine what kind of an animal had pink eyes.

Norah pressed her nose against one of the holes and took a deep breath. She wrinkled her nose and pulled it away quickly. "Yuck! Whatever is in this box has a terrible smell!" she said in disgust. Norah decided that she had best get

Mother before she opened this box.

Mother wasn't far away. She had been standing just around the corner outside Norah's door, listening. "Hi!" she said as she poked her head round the corner. "Smell something funny?"

"I smell something," answered Norah, "but it isn't very funny. It's really kind of yucky!"

"The word is *musky*," said Mother. "That smell coming from the box is a musky smell made by a very funny little animal. Shall I open the box and introduce him to you?"

Norah pulled back from the box. "OK," she said in a quiet little voice. Could someone possibly have given Mother a skunk?

Mother broke the tape and opened the box. Quick as a wink a little white head popped over the top and two little pink eyes blinked at Norah. A little pink nose sat on the end of a funny long snout. Norah saw two little white paws with tiny pink toes grasping the edge of the box.

Norah began to laugh. "That's the funniest skunk I've ever seen!" she said with glee.

"Perhaps that's because it isn't a skunk," said Mother.

Norah laughed even harder when Mother lifted the little animal from the box. Norah saw a long thin body and a long white fluffy tail. Attached to the body were four stubby little legs. "Oh, Mother!" gasped Norah between giggles. "What is it? I've never seen such a strange little animal."

"This is a baby ferret," said Mother. "It is all white and pink because it is an albino ferret. That means that it doesn't have any coloring in its skin and fur. Some ferrets are albino, but they also come in different shades of brown and black."

"He is so cute!" said Norah. She reached out to take the little ferret from Mother. "Wherever did you get it, Mommy?"

But Mother did not let Norah take the ferret from her. "I want to tell you something about this little ferret first," said Mother. "This little fellow came from a pet shop. Some people bought it as a pet for their little boy. But the child was not used to handling animals, especially animals like ferrets. The boy was afraid of the little ferret. When he picked it up, it bit him. That frightened the child so much that he threw the ferret down to the ground. His parents realized that this was not a good pet for him. The boy was afraid of the ferret, and the ferret was afraid of the boy."

Mother turned the baby ferret onto its back and gently stroked its chest as she talked. The ferret blinked its little pink eyes a few times and went to sleep. "An animal can sense when someone is afraid of him," continued Mother. "Then the animal becomes afraid that the person will hurt him. Some frightened animals, like the possum, make believe they are dead. Some animals, like your little hamsters, roll over on their backs with their paws in the air when they're afraid. Most frightened animals will run away if they can. But when a frightened animal is cornered or suddenly picked up by a stranger, he will usually bite. He doesn't bite because he's mean. He bites because he is afraid and is trying to protect himself. That is why you should never try to pick up an animal that you do not know, especially if he is frightened or hurt."

Norah knew all about this rule. She had watched Mother put on long, heavy gloves before picking up most of the little wild animals she cared for. She had seen Mother put heavy towels over larger birds so they couldn't peck her, especially if their beaks were sharp and curved. Sometimes Mother used a strong net to pick up an animal or bird. And there were some animals that Mother would never touch. Instead, she would call the Animal Rescue League. Norah was never allowed to touch any animal until Mother or Father had checked it first.

There was also another important rule about baby birds and baby animals. Mother told Norah that most wild babies she might see by themselves had not been abandoned by their parents. The babies were only waiting while the mother and father were hunting for food or shelter. The parents of these little creatures could do a much better job of caring for them than people could. Norah knew that most baby creatures that are picked up by well-meaning people die because the people really didn't know how to feed or care for them.

Mother gently placed the sleeping ferret into the crook of Norah's arm. Norah petted the little animal with the tip of her finger. The ferret opened his pink mouth and yawned. Norah saw very sharp little white teeth in the ferret's mouth. "Oh!" exclaimed Norah quietly. "This ferret certainly does have sharp teeth! I wouldn't want him to bite me."

"Yes," said Mother. "His teeth are very sharp. But cats and dogs have sharp teeth too. They can bite, but they also can make very good pets if they are treated gently. A ferret also makes a good pet if he is treated with kindness."

Norah looked down at the little animal snuggled in her arm. He had a look of complete peace on his face. She wanted this little ferret to be her friend.

"God did not originally create animals to be cruel," continued Mother. "He created them to be kind and gentle. It is because of sin that animals hunt and kill. Most animals hunt and kill to eat. The do not do it to be mean. They protect themselves and their families by using their teeth and claws. It is sad that sin has changed the animals."

"But someday," said Norah with a gentle smile on her face, "the animals will not be frightened. Someday they will not have to hunt and kill for food. God will make all the animals gentle in heaven."

"Isn't that wonderful!" replied Mother. "The Bible says, 'And the leopard shall lie down with the kid.' I hope that day comes soon, Norah."

"Me too!" exclaimed Norah.

The little ferret became one of Norah's favorite pets. She always treated it with kindness, and the ferret gave her his love in return. Norah kept him in a clean cage at night and for part of the day. She frequently took him out and let him play in the house with her. She gave him the name Weasel because that is what he looked like to her. She played tag and hide-and-seek with Weasel. Sometimes she even took him outside into the garden. He especially liked flowers. He would jump at their bobbing heads. Sometimes he would be quite naughty and pull a flower head off. Norah tried to scold him, but underneath she thought it was cute. She would let him take the flower he picked into the house. How Mother and Norah would laugh when they found Weasel sound asleep on his back with a flower clutched in his front paws!

Norah knew that she had to be very careful when she took Weasel outdoors. He loved to explore. He was so small and thin that he could get into the tiniest of places. He could also slip through the narrow spaces between the board fence. Norah just managed to catch him two or three times when he tried that little trick.

One warm and sunny day Norah took him into the garden while she pulled weeds. Weasel raced round, jumping up at her and pulling the weeds out of her hands. He got to be such a nuisance that she finally put him down inside a deep metal bucket so she could get something done. She placed a small pinecone in the bucket with him to give him something to play with.

Norah weeded and weeded. She forgot about Weasel. She forgot that he was in the bucket. She didn't think about it till she heard Mother calling. Then she went to the bucket to take Weasel out. But Weasel was not in the bucket. The bucket had fallen over, and the pinecone lay on the ground near it. But Weasel was nowhere in the garden!

Norah raced to the house and told Mother. Then she and Mother began to search. They searched through the garden. They searched all over the yard. They searched in the neighbors' yards. They called and called Weasel's name, but he did not come when they called. They could not find the little ferret.

It was a very sad Norah who went to bed that night. She had cried till her throat hurt. How she missed her little white ferret friend! Norah and her parents had prayed for Weasel in worship that evening. She and Mother knelt down by her bed just before she went to sleep and prayed for Weasel again.

They asked Jesus to protect Weasel and to bring him back to them, safe and sound.

Norah and Mother looked for Weasel the next day. They walked from house to house, asking people if they had seen him. Most people had never seen a ferret. Norah carefully described her pet to each person she talked to. Mother left their phone number with each person.

Three days passed. Mother was just getting Norah ready for bed when the phone rang. It was a call from some people who lived four blocks away. They had seen Weasel that evening. He had pressed his little pink nose against a window and looked in at them. They had never seen an animal like that before. The man quickly got his camera and took a picture of Weasel. Later that evening he had called a friend who lived nearer Norah's house. He told the friend about the strange little white animal with the pink nose and the pink eyes. The man's friend remembered the description Norah had given him when she had asked at his house.

Right away Norah and Mother went to the house of the man who had seen Weasel, and called and called. They searched everywhere, but they could not find Weasel.

Six days later Mother and Norah started making signs. The signs read "Lost—a white albino ferret; looks like a small weasel." They put their phone number on all of the signs. Daddy took the signs and drove around the streets near their house. He put them up at every corner. He drove to streets farther from their house and put some signs up. Soon there seemed to be "Lost—ferret" signs for miles around.

Norah, Mother, and Daddy prayed for Weasel every morning and every evening. Norah prayed throughout the day. She asked Jesus to keep Weasel safe and to help him find his way back home.

On the afternoon of the tenth day there was another phone call. A woman who lived three miles away called Norah's house. She said that she had seen all the "Lost-—weasel" signs. She told them that she had gone into her laundry room that afternoon to put her clothes into the washing machine. When she picked up the pile of clothes, a gray animal dropped out and landed on the floor. She saw some white fur on his back and some white fur on his head, but the rest of him was gray. She saw a little pink nose and pink eyes. "I was afraid to pick him up," said the lady. "He is hurt and sick. He has a very bad cut on his back."

Norah and Mother raced to the car and jumped in. They drove to the woman's house. Mother was amazed. They had to cross two wide and busy highways. "How did Weasel cross the highway without getting hit?" asked Mother.

"He could if Jesus protected him," said Norah with a positive expression on her face. "We asked Jesus to protect him, and Jesus did."

At the woman's house Norah and Mother opened the laundry room door very slowly. They peeked inside. Mother had a heavy towel and her long, thick gloves. But Mother didn't need to use the towel or the gloves. Norah ran to her beloved little pet and scooped him up in her arms. He nestled contentedly in the crook of her arm and yawned.

Mother took Weasel to a pet doctor. The doctor washed Weasel and gave him an injection. He told Mother that Weasel's bad cut was infected, and that he had a high fever. The doctor shaved the white fur around the cut and then sewed it up. Weasel had to stay in the pet hospital for two days.

How happy Norah was when Weasel came back home! He had a big patch of fur missing from his back and a big white bandage on. But Weasel was home! He stretched out on his back against the pillows on Norah's bed and went to sleep. Norah went out to the garden and picked a little pink flower. She tiptoed into her room and gently placed the flower in Weasel's paws. Weasel yawned but did not open his eyes. He had a very peaceful look on his face.

A Little Albino Ferret

Weasel's Box House

His Favorite Sleeping Spot

Weasel loved flowers.

God's Promise
and the White Dove

Norah pressed her nose against the cold window. She looked at the gray sky and the big puddles of water in her backyard. Water dripped from the roof of the house and the swaying branches of the trees. Tiny rivers of water ran down the windowpane, making crooked little lines.

Norah had never seen so much rain! It had rained for three days now. There was so much rain that the brook across the street was overflowing its banks and now covered the roadway. Cars could no longer travel up and down Norah's street. She had been shocked to see the two older boys who lived up the street come paddling down the flooded roadway in their canoe.

Norah's mother and daddy were very worried. They were worried that soon the water would get so high that it would come into their house. Norah's house was on the top of a small hill. But the hill was too small now. The rising waters seemed to be gobbling it up, bit by bit.

Norah and her mother and father had been doing a lot of praying. They asked God to keep the water from coming into their house. They asked God to stop the rain. But God did not seem to be answering their prayers very quickly. The rain kept falling, and the water kept creeping up the hill.

Norah tried to draw a picture of the canoe on the wet and hazy windowpane. She drew the heads of the two boys sticking up out of the canoe. It was getting very boring just sitting around in the house. She wanted to go outdoors and splash around in the puddles. But Mother had told her that it was not safe to splash around in the water when there was a flood, even a small flood. She explained to her that the water was often polluted and that there could be snakes that had been washed out of their nests.

Suddenly Norah's attention was drawn to a flash of white in the maple tree. She saw a white object fluttering in the branches. Then the object seemed to flutter down toward the ground. Norah could not tell where it landed. But Norah knew that something was wrong. She quickly called Mother and told her of what she had seen.

Mother pulled on her rubber boots and put on her raincoat and her wide-brimmed rain hat. "Stay in the house, Norah," said Mother. "I will go out and look around under the maple tree. You can watch me from the window." Mother went out the back door and started splashing through the deep puddles. She had to lift her feet high, for there were branches floating around in the water.

Norah watched Mother working her way around the base of the maple tree. Then Mother stopped and reached down for something. She held her arm up, and Norah could see a dripping white object in Mother's hand. Mother tucked the object under her raincoat and came splashing back to the house.

"What did you find, Mother?" asked Norah in an excited voice when Mother opened the back door. A cold spray of water hit Norah's face as she closed the door behind Mother.

"I think it is some kind of white dove," said Mother as she pulled a soggy bird from under her raincoat and layed it in a towel on the table. "I don't think it's a pigeon. It's too small for a pigeon. It has a thin black band of feathers around its neck."

Norah looked at the poor dove. It blinked its little eyes back at her, but it didn't try to move. It didn't even try to stand up on its feet. "Do you think this dove has a cold?" asked Norah.

"Yes," said Mother. "It may even have an infection in its lungs. I don't think this dove is a wild bird. I think that he is someone's pet. He probably lived in a cage in someone's nice warm house. He may have gotten out somehow and gotten lost in all this rain. Now he is cold and wet and sick."

Mother dried the dove in the warm towel, and Norah prepared a special cage for him. She put soft cotton in the bottom and a small light bulb at the top for warmth. Mother opened the dove's mouth and placed a dropperful of medicine inside. The sick dove did not move. It just blinked its eyes.

Mother and Norah were so busy taking care of the dove that they didn't notice that the light coming through the kitchen window was getting brighter. It wasn't till mother went over to the sink to wash out the eyedropper that she noticed a little patch of blue in the sky over the maple tree.

"Let's go outside for a few minutes," Mother said to Norah.

"But why?" asked Norah. "I thought that you didn't want me to go out in the rain."

"I don't think it's raining anymore," said Mother with a twinkle in her eye.

Norah raced to the back door with Mother close behind her. The air felt cool and damp. Norah could smell wet earth and wet trees. But she did not see any raindrops falling. There was a lovely patch of blue sky just over the maple tree. Suddenly bright lines of sunshine pierced through the clouds around the edges of the blue spot. Norah drew in her breath. It looked like gold streamers spreading outward and pushing the clouds away with them. "Mother, have you ever seen such a beautiful sight!" exclaimed Norah.

"There's something even more beautiful in the sky behind you," said Mother in a hushed voice.

Norah turned around, and gasped. There, stretched across the sky directly over their house, was the most beautiful rainbow she had ever seen. There were really two rainbows, a brilliantly colored one below, and just above it a lighter one that seemed to have its colors upside down. "It looks like there is a mirror behind the lower rainbow," said

Norah. "The lighter one is the image in the mirror."

"That's called a double rainbow," said Mother. "And in a way you are right. The lighter-color rainbow above is a reflection of the real rainbow below it. There is so much moisture in the sky that it works like a mirror."

Mother and Norah stood quietly for some time. They could not take their eyes off the beautiful sight in the sky.

"Do you know what?" asked Mother. "God has sent us His promise. Do you remember the story of Noah and the ark?"

"It's one of my favorite stories," Norah reminded Mother.

Mother smiled down at Norah. "How could I ever forget," she said.

Norah tugged on Mother's arm. "I think He sent us another promise, too. Do you remember the white dove that Noah sent out of the ark?"

"Ah, yes," said Mother. "God answered our prayers and sent us two beautiful symbols of His love."

Mother put her arm around Norah's shoulders. "Come on, little one. It's time to go back inside. It is feeding time. It's time to go in and feed Norah's ark of animals!"